Disciples of Jesus

J. C. Wenger

HERALD PRESS
Scottdale, Pennsylvania
Kitchener, Ontario

Scripture quotations in this book are from the Revised Standard Version of the Bible, copyrighted 1946, 1952,© 1971, 1973.

DISCIPLES OF JESUS
Copyright © 1977 by Mennonite Board of Missions
    Elkhart, Ind. 46514
Published by Herald Press, Scottdale, Pa. 15683
    Released simultaneously in Canada by Herald Press,
    Kitchener, Ont. N2G 4M5
Library of Congress Catalog Card Number: 77-86343
International Standard Book Number: 0-8361-1836-7
Printed in the United States of America
Design: Alice B. Shetler/Art by Elmore Byler

10 9 8 7 6 5 4 3 2 1

Distributed overseas by Mennonite Broadcasts, Inc.,
Box 1252, Harrisonburg, Va. 22801.

CONTENTS

PREFACE

Followers of Jesus Christ can be found today all over the world. Among these Christians are Mennonites who take their name from Menno Simons, a Frisian Reformer of the sixteenth century.

Until the nineteenth century, most Mennonites were found in Europe and North America. During the twentieth century, however, mission, relief, and service activities have resulted in a worldwide Mennonite fellowship.

One major emphasis of the Mennonites is to practice daily the teachings of Jesus. This book sets forth some of these teachings as found in the New Testament.

Disciples of Jesus is volume five of the Mennonite Faith Series listed inside the back cover. We hope the material will be of interest to anyone wanting to understand the Christian faith in general and Mennonites in particular.

Anyone wanting to study Mennonite faith and life further may check the references placed at the back of each book.

J. Allen Brubaker

4

1

WHAT IS CHRISTIAN DISCIPLESHIP?

A story is told about a shepherd boy who found a special flower. This flower caused him to find the mouth of a hidden cave containing a vast amount of wealth. The boy was led about the cave by a guide who kept assuring him, "Take all you want!" But seeing that the boy, in his excitement, had dropped the special flower the guide kept saying, ". . . but don't forget the best."

It was necessary for the lad to retain the special flower until he had his new wealth safely out of the cave. But alas, the boy completely forgot the flower. Eventually he awoke from a nap with his hands clutched full of dry leaves.

We can see that the boy lacked discipline. In his joy and excitement, he didn't hear his guide and let his mind stray from the most important thing—the special flower. That's the way it is sometimes with some Christians. They get so excited with worldly things that they lose sight of their leader and the most important values in life.

Christian Discipleship

Christian discipleship means accepting and living out, in daily life, the lifestyle and teachings of Jesus Christ as found in the New Testament. Christian discipleship involves our wills or our "want-to." It asks, "How can I glorify God in my life?"

Christian discipleship is not an "I must," to escape the wrath of God. It is not merely "I will," an attempt to buy the favor of God by good works.

There is always the danger of confusing our Christian behavior and action with our salvation itself. But the Lord wants more than a certain pattern of behavior—strict morality of life, honesty, kindness, sharing with the needy, and the like. Christ wants His disciples to bear the fruit of the Spirit. He wants them to resemble Him as closely as possible in character. But it's impossible for anyone, apart from Christ, to seek to please Him by a good life. It is utterly impossible to be a Christian disciple without accepting His saving work on the cross. Discipleship involves such sorrow for sin that one repents, turns resolutely from sin, and makes a full surrender of himself to the Lord Jesus.

The Mind of Christ

Christian discipleship means having the mind of Christ. After we give ourselves completely to Christ, He gives us His Spirit. Once we have His Spirit, we find ourselves wanting to do His will, not ours. When we have His Spirit, discipleship becomes a "want-to" not an "I must" or "I will."

The Apostle Paul in Romans 8 contrasts the mind of the flesh and the mind of the Spirit. This passage clearly shows the difference between putting one's mind on carnal, fleshly concerns or on the enlarging and upbuilding of the cause of Christ. The Spirit of God seeks to lead each member to build up and to enlarge the body of Christ.

There is a danger that some people will think that the mind of the Spirit produces some sort of long-faced, ascetic piety; that if one is Spirit-filled, he will rarely smile—he will be inflexible, strict, and rigid. Nothing could be farther from reality. It is carnal to be inflexible, rigid, and harsh.

The Spirit-filled person has been set free from negative attitudes. Because he has been fully forgiven and accepted in Christ by grace alone, he is now free to accept and love himself. With the enslaving chains broken, he is now free to be a loving, gracious person, quick to show love, to forgive, and to be ready to believe the best.

A New Authority

We have seen that Christian discipleship means having the mind of Christ and living out in daily life His teachings. It means making Him

Lord of all of life. In other words, Christ is the new source of authority in our lives. The old nature of sin and death no longer controls us. Rather, we are alive with a new nature through Christ and His Spirit. This new force or power gives us the desire to follow Christ and daily live the kind of life Jesus has shown to us as recorded in the four Gospels.

2

EXAMPLES OF CHRISTIAN DISCIPLESHIP

WE can learn much about discipleship by observing disciples. The Gospels and Acts are God-inspired records of the early disciples. We can learn a lot from them, even though we live in a different kind of world.

Our problem is: How do we show discipleship? Let's examine the lives of several disciples of Christ who lived in recent times.

Doris Liechty Lehman (1928-1973)
The married folks of the Belmont Mennonite Church in Elkhart, Indiana, looked forward to a delightful Sunday school class experience with

9

team teachers David G. and Doris L. Lehman. But that was before cancer took Doris' life in 1973.

Doris had lived a satisfying Christian life before marriage. After graduation from Goshen College in 1950, she taught high school at Pettisville, Ohio. In 1951, she and David, the dental student who later became an orthodontist, were married.

After their marriage, they provided leadership in a home for young people in Indianapolis, Indiana. The home was maintained for young men of the church who had been drafted for military service but who had decided to do civilian service instead. Many of the men worked in hospitals under a government provision for conscientious objectors. This provision allowed persons who objected to military service to do work of national importance under civilian direction.

While in Indianapolis, Doris also helped the people of Marion County to enrich their home-life. Later she and her husband moved to Puerto Rico to serve the needs of the people there. Eventually, they settled in Elkhart. Here David set up his denistry practice and Doris served as wife and mother in a home blessed with two sons and four daughters.

Their experiences in Indianapolis and Puerto Rico gave them a rich background from which to relate to the needs of their friends and fellow members at Belmont. Out of these experiences they shared thoughts on the Sunday school lesson and responded to questions. Many people were blessed as they participated in class or ex-
10

perienced the hospitality of the Lehmans' home.

Doris was a woman with vibrant energy. Although a devoted wife and the busy mother of six children, she found time for the women's work of her church. She served for a time as president of the Indiana-Michigan Women's Missionary and Service Commission, and also as president of the national WMSC organization. When Leighton Ford held his evangelistic crusade in northern Indiana, Doris was asked to take charge of the women's prayer groups. She was also active in conducting women's retreats at various points in North America and served on the Overseas Committee of the Mennonite Board of Missions.

When she took ill with cancer in 1972, she felt constrained—for the first time in her life—to cancel a retreat. The theme of the retreat which she could not lead was, "The Life of Faith." During the final year of her life, she lived the life of faith in an unusually rich manner. She died of cancer on September 24, 1973, at the early age of forty-five.

In spite of her many obligations, she gave the impression of being on top of her many assignments. Endowed with exceptional gifts and unusual energy, she found life in Christ and in His body, the church, to be fulfilling and rich. She enjoyed fun, as David and her children can testify.

During her illness she and her companion were, at times, certain that God was going to heal her and raise her up to continue her service. Yet she was also able to surrender to the will of her kind heavenly Father. A few weeks before her

11

death she was hospitalized briefly, but she assured her family that she was "not going to lie depressed" on her hospital bed.

One of her good friends, Verna Troyer, the wife of a Goshen eye specialist (ophthalmologist), wrote: "Did Doris ever struggle with any sense of inadequacy? I don't really know; but we all know that when the big test came to surrender the life she loved so well, she met that test with acceptance and firm testimony to the goodness of God and the rightness of His ways."

Lois Gunden Clemens, editor of the WMSC *Voice*, also commented on the death of Doris: "During the past year our WMSC experienced the loss of a dedicated and beloved leader among us in the death of Doris Lehman. But for Doris, it was not really death to die. Her attitude as she faced death expressed in a remarkable way the following statement by D. Reginald Thomas: 'The answer of the gospel to death is like an incident in life—not some awful, horrible event to be feared and dreaded, but a benediction by which we are brought into full awareness of God, there to know Him as he already knows us.' "

Doris had an older sister, Mary, the wife of a Goshen surgeon, Ernest E. Smucker. She described vividly the last three weeks of her sister's life. She related how Doris wished to be at the table as her family ate the evening meal—even though she herself was too weak to join them in eating. "That's when the fellowship takes place. I can't miss it."

One evening Doris' nine-year-old son, Joe, proudly showed his mother his school paper. It was marked "A," and Doris thought the time had come to prepare him for the coming separation. She said, "Joe, do you know that Mommy is sick enough that she might die and not be here very long?"

Little Joe's eyes widened as he replied, "I didn't know."

Then as a Christian disciple, Doris assured him that God would see that others—his father, his older brother and sisters, his aunts, and many other friends—would take good care of him.

Shortly thereafter, on the last day of his mother's life, Joe's cousin, Julia, was playing with him. Little Joe asked Julia if she would stay for supper. Julia told Joe that his aunts were there and would make him supper.

"Oh, yes," said Joe, "there'll always be somebody to take care of me."

The assurance of Doris, backed by a lifetime of faithful Christian living and teaching, had enabled little Joe to claim the promise his mother had given to him.

Two days before her death, a minister friend called to see her. Partly to encourage her and partly to keep her from trying to speak when she was too weak, he told her Count Tolstoi's story, "What Men Live By." It contains three great truths: We shall live by love. All people are mortal. God will provide. By this time Doris had lost sixty pounds as the cancer destroyed her body. This made her blue eyes look especially large. When the minister finished the story, Doris said earnestly, "I want to go to Jesus"—a beautiful testimony of her faith.

Some time after her death, the bereaved husband and father gathered his six children around him to prepare a testimony to put on the stone which now marks her grave. It reads:

DORIS LIECHTY LEHMAN
Born 1928
Commitment to Christ 1940
Triumphant Entry into Heaven 1973

Finney

An outstanding disciple of the nineteenth century was Charles G. Finney (1792-1875). As a young man—still far from Christ's kingdom—he began to read law. In those days the "bible" of American lawyers was Blackstone's *Legal Commentaries*. Blackstone must have been a very religious man, for his volumes are filled with references to the divine law as found in the Bible. These Bible references were not much help to young Finney, for he had no real knowledge of the Bible. Neither did he know God through Christ. So he bought a Bible to read in his study of law. He wanted to be the best possible lawyer, and according to his legal guide, that meant he must master the divine law! Soon he was spending more time on the divine law than on Blackstone!

His Spiritual Birth

Before long Finney became more interested in the salvation theme of the Bible than in the theme of divine law. In fact, he came under deep conviction for sin. He began to cry to God for

14

mercy, and promised Him that he was going to become His disciple. The crisis came after several days of misery. On the way to his law office on the morning of October 10, 1821, he heard the voice of God asking him, "Will you accept salvation now, today?"

"Yes," he promised, "I will accept it today—or die in the attempt!" So desperate was he to find peace.

He fled to a woods to be alone with God. There, as he prayed and cried aloud for God's mercy, a statement came into his mind: "Then you will call upon me and come and pray to me, and I will hear you. You will seek me and find me; when you seek me with all your heart." He did not know then where the words came from, but later he found them in Jeremiah 29:12, 13.

Finney spent the whole forenoon in prayer and found peace as he claimed the promises of the Word which the Spirit brought to his mind.

His Call to Preach

Christ, by His Spirit, was preparing Finney for an unusual ministry. Immediately he devoted himself to bringing the unsaved into God's kingdom. God worked mightily through Finney so that just a few words would bring sinners to a deep conviction. He said a few words to "Judge" Benjamin Wright, with whom he was reading law. The Judge fled the office and had no peace until he too surrendered to Christ. Soon a halfhearted deacon, who was suing someone in court, stopped in to see Finney. Finney mildly told him, "I am now Christ's servant. Get some-

15

body else to plead your case." The deacon hurried away, made peace with his adversary, and withdrew his case.

His Evangelistic Ministry

About two years later, in 1823, Finney was licensed to preach in the Presbyterian Church and was soon given a small rural pastorate in Jefferson County, New York. His real ministry proved to be evangelism, and he became Mr. Evangelist in America. The heart of this ministry was from 1824 to 1832. Thousands of persons repented of their sins under his eloquent and moving evangelistic sermons.

Eventually, he held brief pastorates in New York City. His life took a new turn—yet with the same concerns and goals—when he became a teacher of theology in Oberlin (Ohio) College in 1835. He served there for forty years—fifteen years as president—until his death on August 16, 1875. He was thirteen days short of 83. Finney helped to make Oberlin an institution from which came Spirit-filled and effective heralds of the glorious gospel of Jesus Christ.

Empowered by Christ

Finney is a beautiful illustration of how Christ called, equipped, and used a humble servant. His own soul was melted by the love of God.

One of the most amazing aspects of Finney's early ministry was the way the Lord's power sustained him physically. Finney kept up a killing pace for years at a time without even seeming to tire. Eventually, however, his overwork wore him down, and he had to start over at a more reasonable pace.

We have seen that Finney made a full surrender and a total consecration of himself to Christ and His service in 1821. Had he not done this, the rest of his life might have been a complete failure as far as Christ's will for him was concerned. Finney also invested his energies well at Oberlin as he sought to prepare the young men of the nation for a soul-winning ministry.

3

EACH DISCIPLE
IS UNIQUE

WE have looked at the life, experience, and witness of two different disciples: Doris Lehman and Charles Finney. In many ways they could not have been more opposite. Their experience as Christians was as different as was their make-up and nature. In other words, each was unique—one of a kind. Christ by His Spirit gave completely different experiences to each of these disciples, and so neither could judge or condemn the other for what he/she experienced or didn't experience. Christ enabled each one to be the best possible witness for her/his Lord.

And so it is with you. It is your responsibility

each day to be a submissive and yielded disciple of Christ. You do this by opening up your heart and life for the Spirit to mold you more perfectly into the spiritual image of the Lord Jesus. You will want to achieve new levels of control over your temper, new victory over any moodiness which may be a weak point in you. You will seek every day for victory over love of possessions, over self-will, over jealousy, over grudges, over lust, and over any other temptation to be less than Christlike.

A mature Christian character does not develop in a flash. No past "heavenly" experience of Spirit-filling, or the nearness of Christ, or an unusual display of the hand of God in answer to prayer is going to answer your needs today. You must keep filled with the Spirit. Then you will mature as a unique disciple of Christ. You will not need to be like some other Christian.

Grow in Grace

Disciples who follow their Lord move forward under His lordship. They "grow in grace." When faced with a crisis situation, Christians usually take definite forward steps. At such a time, the Christian can either lose ground spiritually by not meeting the conditions for a divine infilling, or he can step to higher ground in Christ, being victorious "in the Spirit." So what are sometimes spoken of as "works of grace" are really true. Conversion is a work of grace. Learning the lesson of trust in a vivid way is a work of grace. Learning to take the mind off the flesh and to put it on the things of the Spirit is a work of grace—

actually, a continuing work of grace. We grow—or fail to grow—as we respond in the Spirit.

We can never, of course, afford to measure ourselves by each other (2 Corinthians 10:12). Instead, each Christian accepts the Lord's dealing with him by the Spirit. Luther once remarked with some wit that if God did not chasten us, we would "snore ourselves to death." The Lord knows which temptations to guard us from and which ones to allow to trouble us. Through difficulties we learn to consciously depend on Him for His keeping power. Here are several examples of persons who through the Spirit grew in grace.

Heshbon Mwangi

When Heshbon Mwangi of Kenya confessed Christ, he became a new man. Things he had stolen he returned to their owners. He went to the elders of the church, asked forgiveness, and told them what God had saved him from. He even arranged to have a Christian wedding with his wife.

Although he and young John Kambaro, who had won him to Jesus, taught in schools some miles apart, they met after school every evening to fellowship and to witness to the other teachers.

At the time there were only two others in the area who were "on fire for Jesus," the one fifteen miles away and the other seven miles distant. But the four of them got together every two or three days. They were zealous believers and spoke to everyone. The people got tired of their witnessing. They became so angry they thought they could kill them.

One day in June 1942 some young fellows caught Heshbon and knocked him unconscious. While a lot of others watched, his attackers beat him and beat him, but he didn't feel it because he was unconscious. Some even wanted to kill him, but they stopped short of murder. Finally, he regained consciousness. Slowly he got up on his knees. Then he examined his attitudes to see if he had hate for these who tried to kill him.

To his great surprise he found none. His jaws were swollen shut so that he couldn't speak. Yet, he prayed for them silently, "Father, forgive them, they really didn't know what they were doing." His heart was full of love. As he slowly got to his feet, he looked with love at each of the young men. He looked them in the eye and just loved them. They pointed the way to his home. He started very slowly, trembling and wobbling, on the road to his home.

Heshbon's wife and mother took care of him when he got home.

Three days later he went back to the village where he was beaten. He acted as if nothing happened. He said, "Fellows, tomorrow I am going to plaster my mother's house. Won't you come and help me?" Because of Heshbon's love they came and helped. Two or three days later one of the fellows came to Heshbon and said, "I knocked you out. I am sorry. I need Jesus. Please hit me hard to help pay my debt."

Heshbon said, "No, I can't give Satan room like that. [As a believer] I'm afraid to fight, but I wish you'd take Jesus."

The man prayed, but didn't go on with God.

21

However, another of those men came and turned to Jesus. He was saved. This was the beginning— the time of fruit had come. After the beating, school pupils, a teacher, and some people of the community turned to Jesus. Heshbon's wife praised the Lord. Their home became a center where those who loved Jesus loved to come.

In 1952 Heshbon was headmaster of a large primary school. At the time, hundreds and hundreds of Kikuyu people in central Kenya had turned to Jesus. Heshbon was concerned for many of them who recently had come to Jesus and needed shepherding. He decided that at the end of the year he would give all his time to God's work, to care for those who had become Christians.

These Kikuyu believers faced a big problem. For two years their tribe had been caught up in a massive resistance movement against the government—full of violence and hate and robbery. The resisters called themselves "Mau Mau," and a large segment of the tribe were living in hideaways in the forests. Schools were being taken over, police stations ambushed and robbed. Those of the tribe who refused to cooperate with the terrorists were murdered or threatened. Fear stalked the land.

Heshbon heard that they wanted to turn his school into a resistance school.

One evening as he was reading in bed, somebody pounded on his door with a big knife. "Who's there?" he shouted. "Me," someone said.

"Well, don't do that anymore!" He rose

quickly, went to the door, and opened it. The man ran away. A group of men stood on the road. Nothing further happened that evening, but he had in his house all the money to pay the wages for the six teachers in his school.

In the morning, with all this cash in a bag, he went to school on his bicycle. He noticed groups of people standing along the road watching him and muttering. He didn't know that they had sent for the Mau Mau to attack him. When he reached the school, the teachers were standing in a group talking; the children were all lined up, ready for inspection.

"Good morning, teachers. How are you?" he asked. "Fine," they said.

He took the money into the office, locked it up, and came back out for inspection. But men ran in, quickly grabbed him, overpowered him, and began beating him. They had knives and pistols.

As they beat him they asked, "Who is Jesus?"

He said, "Jesus is the Son of God and my Savior."

"Can't you say you are one of us?"

Heshbon said, "No, I belong to Jesus."

They beat him unmercifully. "Give us the money!"

"I have none here."

They slashed his face; his blood flowed freely.

"Don't you know that Jesus is a white man?"

"No," said Heshbon, "He is the Son of God."

"Jesus is an Asian."

"No, He is the Son of God and my Savior. He will be yours, too, if you will receive Him."

"Kill him!" said one. "Shoot him."

He said, "Wait a bit. I have nothing against you. Only that I love Jesus."

The teachers had been threatened and they just stood there. Pupils were crying, and running away. They loved their teacher, and they thought he would surely die.

Heshbon was all alone. He was badly cut. They searched him for money, but found only his Bible. "What's this book?"

"That's Jesus' book."

So they knocked out his teeth.

Then one said, "Let's not kill him. Let him teach the children." Miraculously the men began to leave him, perhaps to look for the money. From the ground he called, "I forgive you for my blood that you spilled and for my teeth. I forgive and I will pray for you!"

One came back and tramped on him. Again, the man said, "Let him go on teaching the children."

They broke into the office, took the money, and left.

After some time Heshbon struggled to his feet. All the pupils had run, spreading the news that their teacher had been killed. The teachers were stunned and helpless. Heshbon staggered painfully to the local dispensary. But there wasn't much anyone could do.

He started for home and was greatly relieved to be met by two brothers who had come as fast as they could on their bicycles. They heard that he had been killed and had come to pick up his body for burial.

They said, "Brother! You are alive!"

He said, "I have Jesus."

The English District Officer then came along in his car and picked him up. He wrote a check to replace the stolen wages and took Heshbon home to his wife, who was sorrowing at the news of his death. Then a missionary came and took him to a large hospital for X-rays. His skull was not fractured, so they took him to one of their homes and nursed him back to strength and health.

Two and one-half weeks later he was asked, "Would you like to transfer to another school?"

"No," he said, "I want to go back to tell them about Jesus, and to witness to the schoolchildren till the end of the year."

"You will be killed," the people said.

"No, I don't have any hate for anyone at all."

He realized that God had given him a very wonderful love for the attackers even though he didn't know who they were. The government messenger came with forms to fill out for compensation for the loss of his teeth, but he refused. He said, "I don't want compensation. I fully forgive them and have forgotten it."

Later, amazingly, by God's grace, he was given dentures. Heshbon says, "Now I can eat and laugh." He laughs with the joy of Jesus, but the deep scars on his face and body will remain. [*]

Suhadiweko Djojodihardjo

About the year 1950 the General Council of

[*]From the Foundation Series story collection, used by permission of The Publishing Council. The Foundation Series.

the North American Mennonite Church was in session in the Hotel Atlantic in Chicago. Into the meeting walked mission leader Orie O. Miller, accompanied by an impressive brother from the island of Java. This brother had gone through very difficult times—German occupation, Muslim persecution, Japanese occupation. Because of these difficulties, even the future of the Javanese Mennonite Church was in question. (Over the years Orie came to call this Javanese brother "Hadi" from a part of his first name. But most Mennonites around the globe used the first two syllables of his last name, pronounced in English, "Jo-yo.") God used "Jo-yo" (more properly, Djojo) in a mighty way to sustain and strengthen the weakened church in Java.

Djojo is a fourth-generation Christian. His great-grandfather turned to Christianity under the ministry of the Dutch Mennonite missionaries who came to Java in 1851. (Java is one of three thousand Indonesian islands scattered over an enormous stretch of ocean.) Djojo's own father, Sardjo Djojodihardjo, was a teacher and pastor and a man of much prayer. Young "Hadi" attended the village schools from age six to fourteen. He then went to high school at Semarang, and finally to seminary in Djakarta. During his seminary training he entered a period of severe doubt. So great was his distress of soul that he was about to give up what little faith he still had and drop out of school. In this crisis he called upon God with great earnestness, and the Lord strengthened him in a vision. This vision greatly increased Djojo's faith, and he finished his

26

studies with great joy. He then married a lovely companion, Armini, and their union was blessed with six daughters and a son.

The years immediately after his marriage were the most difficult because of the political situation—and famine! Djojo was closely watched by the police, and he would probably have been put to death except for the gracious hand of God upon him. Part of the time he was in hiding; at times he and his family almost starved. But God had a great work for Djojo, and always brought him and his family through their difficulties. God also used the times of danger and difficulty to teach him and Armini how great, how good, and how faithful He is. During this time of hiding, Djojo read the Old Testament through twice, and the New Testament four times.

Eventually, Djojo was appointed to the presidium of the Mennonite World Conference. He is an accomplished linguist, speaking Dutch, German, French, and English fluently, in addition to his mother tongue. But the contribution he makes at home and around the globe is not based on his ability in various languages nor on his intellectual gifts nor on his theological insights. It is rather his prayer life. People from far and near in Indonesia come to him for help with their problems, including their illness. It is a great joy for him to kneel in fervent prayers of intercession. And God has been pleased to hear those prayers on many occasions, with amazing deliverances and healings. Djojo, therefore, believes that the church can still expect miracles similar to those described in the Book of Acts,

27

when God's children trust him and cry to Him for help.

For example, in 1971 many members of the Presidium of the Mennonite World Conference attended the Southeast Asia Mennonite Conference held at Dhamtari, MP, India. One day a sick brother came to the porch where the Presidium itself was meeting. He spoke quietly to Djojo, who then excused himself briefly. The brother was a diabetic and medicine could not bring his blood sugar level down to normal. Djojo prayed with him, and sent him to the hospital for a checkup. His blood sugar level was then a bit below the average!

Djojo has been the head of the church in Indonesia for over a quarter century. Those associated with him are impressed with his happy Christian spirit, his warm heart of love, and his humility. Never is he heard reciting all the miracles God has been pleased to perform through him. For example, in Indonesia it is reported that he has been used of the Lord to restore life to a dead man. If Djojo is asked about it, he says that he simply does not know whether or not the man was dead. The man had lain out in a field for a day or two, apparently dead, with ants crawling in and out of his mouth. In answer to prayer, however, he was revived.

All Christians know that God is sovereign. He knows best whom to heal, and who can best glorify Him by death. Leon C. Yoder, a Mennonite Central Committee worker in Indonesia, is an example of the latter. Lee was struck with melanoma, an especially dangerous form of

28

cancer. On more than one occasion Djojo was about to pray for the healing of Leon, but somehow the Spirit of God directed his thoughts so that the words did not come out at all as the man Djojo had intended. Instead of asking for Leon's healing, Djojo found himself praying that God might be glorified through this illness—a prayer that was marvelously answered.

The humble spirit of Djojo became evident to those attending the Amsterdam sessions of the Mennonite World Conference held in 1967. The Resolutions Committee on which Djojo was serving was working on a resolution to bring before the entire assembly. An early draft of the resolution recognized the fruitful way the Holy Spirit was blessing the congregations of Christ's people in various lands, "especially in some of the younger churches." At the request of Djojo, that last clause was deleted. "It might look," he said thoughtfully, "like He is not blessing the older churches!"

A. H. Unruh

We shall look at one more Spirit-filled man as we seek to observe how Christ blesses and uses His disciples. A. H. Unruh (1878-1961) was born in the Crimea, South Russia. His father died young—after asking A. H. to serve as "father" in the family. A. H. attended common school, high school, and normal school in Russia until 1895 when he became a schoolteacher. Converted in his latter teens, he was baptized in a stream at eighteen. In 1900, he and Katherine Toews, also of the Crimea, were married. God blessed them with five sons and three daughters. Beginning in 1911 he taught in a school of commerce for seven years, in high school for two years, and in a Bible school for four years.

A Teacher of the Word

Unruh and family managed to emigrate to Canada in 1924, where he immediately became principal of the Winkler (Manitoba) Bible School. Later he became a distinguished professor in the Mennonite Brethren Bible College in Winnipeg. In the United States he earned a Bachelor of Theology degree at Tabor College, and was awarded a Doctor of Divinity degree by Bethel College, a General Conference Mennonite institution. For a number of years, he was the chairman of the Mennonite Brethren General Conference (1936-39). Ordained a minister in Russia in 1904, he became widely known as a most effective teacher of the Word. He was especially strong in interpreting the Bible and Christian faith. One leader in the Mennonite Brethren Church, Henry J. Wiens, described A. H. Unruh as "perhaps the most widely known teacher, preacher, Bible expositor, and public speaker in Mennonite Brethren circles both in Canada and in the United States.

He Walked with God

Those who sat under the teaching and preaching ministry of A. H. Unruh realized that here was a man who knew the Lord, who walked with God, who was filled with the Spirit. He was concerned that his Bible and theology students learn more than dates and doctrines. He preached a Christianity that seized the whole person—heart, soul, and mind. His ministry was so effective because he walked closely with the Lord; he and his Lord were on "speaking terms." For him the Bible was the Word of God written, the very oracles of God. To him the Word had an authority which is absolutely unique for the individual believer and disciple and for the church.

Around the World

We have reviewed the lives of several persons who helped to build the church. In every land there are countless other saints who lived noble lives of devotion to God and service to the church.

In this century, Christ has been blessing Mennonite disciples around the world with both the rich fruit of the Spirit and the gifts of the Spirit. In Indonesia, God is granting remarkable healings in answer to prayer, and the church is growing rapidly through the work of the Holy Spirit. The believers there do not think this is because they are more holy than the older sister churches in other parts of the world. It is rather because the Indonesian believers have laid hold on the power of God by simple faith in Jesus, and the Lord by His Spirit has been most gracious. The churches in Africa are also receiving new believers faster than leaders can be trained, as in parts of Tanzania and Kenya. The church in Latin America has begun sending out missionaries to neighboring countries; from Argentina to Bolivia, for example.

Unique Gifts

The New Testament is clear that the Holy Spirit gives different gifts to members in the body of Christ. Those gifts are given out to each disciple as He wills (1 Corinthians 12:11). It is, of course, wholly inappropriate for one believer to look with jealousy on the gifts received by another, for the Holy Spirit of God knows what He is doing and why. So after reviewing the rich gifts God had given the church at Corinth, the apostle writes (1 Corinthians 12:29, 30): "Are all apostles? [The Greek has a particle which means, Surely not!] Are all prophets? [Surely not!] Are all teachers? [Surely not!] Do all work miracles? [Surely not!] Do all possess gifts of healing? [Surely not!] Do all speak with tongues? [Surely not!] Do all interpret? [Surely not!]" Thus, we see that the Spirit gives different gifts to each member in the body of Christ. On the other hand, the Spirit blesses every believer with the fruit of the Spirit. In today's language that means: love, joy, peace, patience, kindness, goodness, faithfulness, gentleness, and self-control (Galatians 5:22, 23).

We have already seen that discipleship means more than just bearing the name of Christ. Being a true disciple of Christ means following Him in daily life. And this sometimes brings suffering and even death.

4

A DISCIPLE PAYS
THE PRICE

DISCIPLESHIP takes place in the context of life, whether one lives in India, Japan, Tanzania, Zaire, Nigeria, Trinidad, or Argentina. Discipleship is a little like a test. The Christian is tested within himself in his daily round of duties, among his brethren, and in his service to others. These tests vary according to one's own personality, as we have seen. Each person's tests or temptations are also peculiar to his own society and culture.

Some of these tests are similar, but others are not. In one country the test may be in the form of one's allegiance to government; in another, one's attitude toward the largest, most influential religion. In time of war, one's attitude toward killing may be tested.

Disciples Take Up the Cross

Jesus clearly stated that if anyone wishes to be His disciple he must take up his cross and follow Him (Luke 9:23). Dietrich Bonhoeffer, a twentieth-century German theologian, summarized this truth by saying, Jesus bids us come and die! The cross was a symbol of a shameful death, the death of a felon. And that was the "cup" which the Savior had to drink. Being truly human, He shrank from it as He prayed in the Garden of Gethsemane before His arrest. Yet we observe the victory of the Son of Man in the Garden: He ended His prayer in utter submission: "Not what I will, but what thou wilt" (Mark 14:36).

The Savior had to leave Jerusalem on Good Friday, carrying the very cross on which He was to be crucified. So we believers—if we are to be His true disciples, His true followers—must also take up our individual crosses. The believer's "cross" is a symbol of our readiness to bear reproach, persecution, and even death for being His disciple, for following Him, for living as He taught.

Disciples Avoid Lukewarmness

The more lukewarm a professing disciple is, the more favorably worldy minded people will think of him. When he violates the holy law of God as they do, they think well of him. "He may profess to be a Christian, but he is no fanatic, like some of them!"

The more faithful the Christian is, the less sinners will like him. They may say, "He is a radical person, insisting on his odd way of life. We do not care to have him around too much. He makes us uncomfortable! He acts as if a person has to give up every little worldly pleasure if he wishes to be 'saved'—whatever that is!"

The early disciples made men feel like sinners. That is why persecution broke out against Peter, John, Stephen, and against the early church in Jerusalem (Acts 4—8). It is the reason Saul (Paul) of Tarsus raged as he did against the disciples of the Lord: they made him unhappy, so that he felt as if he were kicking against goads (Acts 26:14). These people kept witnessing about a crucified Jewish Teacher as if He were some sort of god; they even insisted on His deity! "Away with such nonsense," cried Saul.

Discipleship Is Costly

Whatever the time, culture, or circumstance of history, discipleship is costly. Christians face the same troubles all mankind faces. Christian disciples sometimes become ill, they experience accidents of all kinds, and they are sometimes victims of evil men. Yet, the Word of God assures Christians that God is sovereign. God is able to restrain evil. He is a God of providence. He watches over His children, and when He allows difficulties to overtake them, He does it for their spiritual growth. Sometimes their suffering advances His cause and kingdom.

Examples of Suffering
Job Suffers for God

Hundreds of years before Christ, a man named Job lived in the land of Uz in the Syrian desert. He was a righteous man, a person of integrity before God. His trust was in the Lord. He was not an open sinner, neither was he a hypocrite. He loved the Lord, and made sacrifices for his sin regularly—also for the sin of his children. A good and devout saint, Job's confidence and trust was in the Lord.

But look what happened to him! One day a servant hastened to Job to report that the Sabeans had carried off his oxen and asses, and killed all the caretakers except himself. While he was yet speaking, another servant rushed up to report that the fire of God (perhaps lightning) had destroyed his flock of sheep and had killed all the shepherds except himself. Before he was through telling the tragedy, still a third servant came to report that three bands of Chaldeans had captured the camels and killed all the camel drivers but himself. And while he was still speaking a fourth messenger came to report that a terrible wind had destroyed the residence of his oldest son, killing all Job's sons and daughters. As if that were not enough, Job broke out with loathsome sores which covered him from head to foot.

Job's wife collapsed under this terrible set of blows. She told Job to curse God and die. But Job was able to bow and yield to that which the Almighty had allowed to come upon him. Job did not know why all this was going on. However, he still believed that God was in control of his life and destiny.

The children of God usually don't know why evil is allowed to befall them. The human tendency is to ask why. The really important thing, however, is to continue to believe that there is a God in control of history, that He is directing our lives.

Had Job's wife dared to believe that God was still in control of their lives, was still the sovereign Lord, she, too, could have supported the faith and the submission of patient Job. This confidence in the sovereignty and the goodness of God Almighty enables Christians to accept whatever evil He allows to befall them. Thus, the Christian can say, "God has a good purpose in allowing this to happen to me! I'll try to discover His will through it."

Saul Endures Hardship for Christ

Saul lived in the first century. The story of his conversion on the Damascus road is well known. Jesus addressed him by name in Aramaic, his mother tongue, "Why are you persecuting me?" In absolute confusion and terror, Saul replied: "Who are you, Lord [or Sir]?" And the answer came back, "I am Jesus whom you are persecuting!" Saul did a lot of praying, and soon the Lord saw that he was now ready to be a disciple and to receive baptism. So He arranged for Ananias to restore his sight, to baptize him into Christ and His body, and to set his feet on the pilgrim road. This road would bring him many difficulties and obstacles. Jesus said of Saul, "I will show him

37

how much he must suffer for the sake of my name" (Acts 9:16).

Saul (in Greek, Paul) was not disobedient to the heavenly vision (Acts 26:19), but set out with great energy to "preach Christ" in the Jewish synagogues (Acts 9:20). Imagine how the Jews must have turned on him with the same fury he had earlier felt against the Christian disciples! Indeed, in a matter of days they made a plot to kill him (Acts 9:23). Paul's days of worldly honor and glory were over.

Many years later, Paul mentioned briefly some of the trials which the world had showered upon him after he took up the cross of a disciple: he had to endure hunger and thirst, to wear rags, to be brutally treated, to be without a home (1 Corinthians 4:11). And in even more detail: he had to endure troubles, hardships, distresses; he had to undergo beatings, imprisonments, riots; he had to do hard work and endure sleepless nights and physical hunger (2 Corinthians 6:4, 5). Paul says he worked much harder than the false prophets. He had been in prison more often than they. He had been beaten more severely. He had been exposed to death time and again. Five times he received from the Jews the legal thirty-nine lashes. Three times he was beaten with rods. One time he was stoned (and left for dead). Three times he suffered shipwreck in the service of Christ. Once he spent a day and a night in the sea. "Who is weak, and I am not weak?" (2 Corinthians 11:29). Such suffering seems to be especially severe when Christ is penetrating a new culture with the gospel. It is thought Paul was eventually beheaded for his faith.

Since the time of Christ, many of His disciples have been killed because of their faith in Him. This was especially true during the sixteenth-century reformation. And perhaps no group suffered martyrdom more than the Anabaptists. They began to live and to teach all the teachings of Jesus and the apostles. And because of their unusual discipleship, they were imprisoned, tortured, and martyred.

Menno Simons Takes up His Cross

One of the most effective leaders and writers in the Anabaptist churches of the sixteenth century was Menno Simons (1495/96-1561) of Friesland, a part of the Netherlands. In 1554 Menno looked back to his easy life prior to his conversion. Although he had been a priest for over eleven years, he now admitted that he was then not a converted person. He did not truly know Christ. In those days, he says, "Everyone sought and desired me; the world loved me and I loved the world. It was said that I preached the Word of God and was a good fellow!"

In the spring of 1535, Menno surrendered himself to Christ. For some months he did his best to preach the Word of God in purity from his Catholic pulpit. But after about nine months, he decided he could no longer remain within the Catholic Church. So he renounced all his worldly reputation and fame, his unchristian abominations, his masses, infant baptism, and easy life. He then willingly submitted to distress and poverty under the heavy cross of Christ. The date on which Menno renounced the Catholic Church was Sunday, January 30, 1536. He then went "underground." That is, he went into hiding, lest he be put to death.

About January 1537 Menno was ordained to the office of elder (now bishop) by request of the peaceful Anabaptists of the Netherlands, the Obbenites. Menno had not wished to serve as an elder. He felt that he was unworthy of the office, and feared the persecution which would likely come should he accept. However, the Obbenites kept begging Menno to become their elder. Menno's own conscience made him uneasy, because he saw their great need for a leader. Menno later wrote, "I surrendered myself soul and body to the Lord, and committed myself to His grace, and commenced in due time, according to the contents of His holy Word, to teach and to baptize, to till the vineyard of the Lord with my little talent, to build up His holy city and temple, and to repair the tumble-down walls" (*Complete Writings*, 672).

This testimony of Menno Simons reflects the heart of a true disciple—whether preacher or farmer or shopkeeper or teacher or factory-worker or physician. Our "secular" work is secondary (although we seek ever to render a credible service "in the name of Christ"). It is the building of the divine kingdom for which we live. Outstanding saints from Polycarp to Wesley to those of today have thought of Christian discipleship in this way.

Menno did not want the pastors to become "professional"—to seek for the recognition of a special class in the church and community, to be afraid to work with their hands. He wanted them to be brothers in the midst of other brothers and sisters. He was quite frank in advising them to rent a farm and milk cows, or to learn a trade. (See *Complete Writings,* 451.)

The state church clergy, however, were professionals in every sense of the word. "They suffer themselves to be greeted as lords and masters; notwithstanding it is forbidden by the mouth of the Lord. Tell me, good reader, did you ever hear or read that the holy apostles and prophets aspired to such high, vain names as do the learned ones and the preachers of the world? The word Rabbi or Master was used of the ambitious scribes and Pharisees but not of the apostles and prophets. Nor do we read of Doctor Isaiah or Master Ezekiel or Lord Paul or Lord Peter. . . . This I write that you may know that such ambitious, proud spirits can never rightly teach you the disdained word of the cross. . . .

"Teachers and preachers who are sent of God are born of God, are of godly nature, and are driven [motivated] by the Spirit of the Lord; they are taught in the things of the kingdom of heaven; they are pressed into the vineyard of the Lord by the pure, unfeigned love of God and of their neighbors. They seek not the gifts of Balak, nor the tables of Jezebel. They seek the praise of God, and the salvation of their souls, and commend their physical needs to Him, who according to the word of His promise cares for the need of all creatures upon earth" (*Complete Writings,* 508-511).

"He who purchased me with the blood of His love, and called me, who am unworthy, to His service, knows me. He knows that I seek not wealth nor possessions nor luxury nor ease, but only the praise of the Lord, my salvation, and the salvation of many souls. Because of this, I with my poor, weak wife and children have for eighteen years endured excessive anxiety, oppression, affliction, misery, and persecution. At the peril of my life I have been compelled everywhere to drag out an existence in fear. Yes, when the [state church] preachers repose on easy beds and soft pillows, we [free-church people] generally have to hide ourselves in out-of-the-way corners. When they at weddings and baptismal banquets revel with pipe, trumpet, and lute, we have to be on our guard when a dog barks for fear the arresting officer has arrived. When they are greeted as doctors, lords, and teachers by everyone, we have to hear that we are Anabaptists, 'bootleg' [unauthorized by the state] preachers, deceivers, and heretics, and be saluted in the devil's name. In short, while they are gloriously rewarded for their services with large incomes and good times, our recompense and portion must be fire, sword, and death" (*Complete Writings*, 674).

Loyal Bartel Paid the Price

In 1901 Minister H. C. Bartel and wife, Mennonite Brethren missionaries, were on their way to China when their first son was born on November 23. They were at sea when the baby arrived. Perhaps the Lord led them to the choice of the right name, Loyal Houlding Bartel. While very young, Loyal gave his life to Christ and dedicated himself wholly to Him. At 19, Loyal returned to the United States to study at Moody Bible Institute, Fort Wayne Bible College, and Northern Baptist Seminary. On June 4, 1926, he married Susan Schultz. They had five children.

Loyal and Susan went to China in 1927 to invest their lives in the building of His kingdom there. He taught in a Bible school, served as an evangelist, and organized Christian congregations.

All sorts of difficulties beset the work in the 1940s. In 1948, Susan and the children returned to the States. Loyal felt compelled by the love of Christ to remain with his brothers and sisters in the faith who were destined to pass through severe affliction. He felt that he wanted to be with them. So he stayed on.

Likely he was not able to do much direct teaching. But he provided a Christian presence, and his brothers and sisters in Christ knew why he remained. In 1966 he wrote:

A few days ago there was a rumor of what might happen, and for more than a half day I was perplexed and fearful, until the thought came to me that we must never doubt the love of God in Christ Jesus towards us. So my heart reposed once more in perfect peace, resting in His everlasting love. How often we are troubled with the thoughts of what might happen, and our hearts cry out like Jesus did, "Oh, that this cup might pass from me," but then we must rest in His will which is based in His love.

The next year, 1967, he wrote:

Sometimes I feel like I am just "marking time" and getting nowhere, but then again there are bright spots.

Uncertainty is everywhere but how glad [I am that] we can rest in the everlasting arms of Him who changes not and to whom there are no unexpected surprises.

So far as is known, Loyal Bartel was the only Protestant missionary to remain in mainland China in this long period, 1948-1971. Death seems to have come to him from illness the summer of 1971. . . . Surely his parents gave him the right name, for he was in very truth a loyal disciple of Jesus Christ, a disciple who put his hand to the plow and never looked back (Luke 9:62).

Summary

In this chapter, we have noted that true disciples take up the cross of their Lord. They avoid halfhearted obedience to Christ, and instead give themselves wholeheartedly to Christ. We have noticed that this kind of radical discipleship is costly because it is in opposition to Satan and to ungodly men and women. We have examined briefly the lives of several persons for whom discipleship was costly. Likely you can think of many other persons who are obediently following Christ in daily life.

5

GUIDELINES FOR
DISCIPLES

ALL through the teaching of Christ—indeed all through the New Testament—the theme of living by love appears again and again. Love in the sense Jesus meant is far more than trying to have a warm feeling for people. A far greater meaning is that we identify so fully with those in difficulty, suffering, or need that we get under their load with them. Jesus told the story (Luke 10) of the traveler who fell among robbers on the Jericho road to describe this kind of love. When we see a person who needs help we do not pass by on the other side. We bind up his wounds, pouring in such healing agents as oil and wine. Then we put him on our beast of burden, and convey him to a pleasant bed in the inn.

Live Love

In our world there are many Jericho roads and many robbers. Racial minorities are crying for justice, for the right to live with human dignity. They want the opportunity to provide decent food and clothing and housing for their families. Prisoners are wasting away in their lonely cells, full of fear and without hope. Many haven't even one caring friend to reach out helping hands of love to them. (The references to prisoners in the New Testament may well mean suffering for one's faith. But political prisoners and criminals are also persons with the need for love, for someone to care about them.) It is not enough to provide food, housing, and some secular recreation. Prisoners need someone who can listen to their story of sorrow, someone to hold their hand as they weep, someone to pray with them. Even loving letters to prisoners can be bright rays of sunshine in the gloom of their boring cells. True disciples need to live love.

The natural disasters of this world—floods, fires, earthquakes, tornadoes—often lead to famine, the need for shelter and medicine. In such disasters, many hands of love should reach out.

Slums in almost all the great cities of the world are places of need. People with creative minds, filled with compassion, are needed to lessen the grinding poverty and the awful evils which are bred in such circumstances.

With all these needs about him, a compassionate Christian cannot think first and always about his own wealth and welfare. He must show concern for the cries of suffering children and the silent tears of the aged who are hurting from cold neglect.

The greatest need of all is, of course, the need for the good news of the gospel. Every person in the world needs to know how to get rid of his load of guilt, how to obtain forgiveness for his sins. He must know how to be reconciled to God, how to have Him as his accepting and caring Father, how to attain that state of spiritual well-being known in Scripture as "salvation." The most urgent problem of mankind is the sin problem. And there is only one answer to that need: the gospel of our Lord Jesus Christ.

Live in Holiness

In the New Testament, to be holy is to be like Jesus. Holiness is yielding to the promptings of the Spirit of God to conform in heart and life as closely to the character of Christ as is humanly possible. The New Testament epistles often begin by praising God for all that He has done for His children—providing Christ as their sacrifice for sin, calling them into His kingdom, blessing them with every spiritual blessing, giving such gifts as He sees are needed in the church, and so on. *Ephesians* is a perfect example. After a brief greeting, the Apostle Paul almost sings as he writes his "Hymn of Redemption," (1:3-14). Notice the three stanzas in these verses: (1) chosen by the Father, (2) redeemed by the Son, and (3) sealed by the Spirit. He stresses the union of believing Jews with believing Gentiles in the church. Following three chapters on the spiritual standing of the believers, Paul turns in the latter half of the epistle to "the walk" of the Christian. The Christian's "walk" is his daily conduct.

Using the figure of taking off dirty clothes, the apostle asks his readers to "lay aside" the old corrupt nature, and to "put on" the new divine nature. Then he describes in some detail what actual separation from sin involves. Putting on the new nature involves: truthfulness (4:25), a controlled temper (4:26), being on the alert against sin (4:27), strict honesty (4:28), pure speech (4:29), a holy life (4:30), overcoming sins of the spirit [such as pride, envy, grudges, jealousy, hostility] (4:31), being Christlike in spirit (4:32), imitating God Himself in character (5:1), and following Christ's law of love (5:2).

Avoid Sin

Paul's list of sinful behavior in Ephesians is less than half the length of those virtues we are to cultivate. We are to avoid: sex sins and greed (5:3), impure speech (5:4), and keeping company with the ungodly (5:7). Before going on to his last negative point, he stresses the positive once more: Be sure to "walk in the light"—that is, in goodness, righteousness, and truth (5:8-10). Finally, he says, "Shun the works of darkness," that is, sin (5:11-13).

Live in Trust

Jesus was aware how human beings tend to worry. He saw living in anxiety as utterly unnecessary. The Father cares for the birds of the air, will the same Father not care for us? Can worry and fretting provide any real help? Our heavenly Father knows our needs and delights to answer our petitions. Can we not believe that He will supply our needs?

All through His ministry, Jesus tried to assure His disciples that they could indeed live without anxiety. It was they who were worried about food for the Four Thousand (Mark 8) and the Five Thousand (Mark 6). He didn't worry; rather, He showed the disciples that because He was the Son of God He could provide, just like the Father. When the dreadful storm arose on the lake, the disciples were beside themselves with fear, while Jesus was so unconcerned that He slept until they wakened Him (Mark 4). After He calmed the storm, He asked, "Why are you afraid? Have you no faith?" (Mark 4:40). How hard it is for us human beings to learn to pray always, rather than to lose heart (Luke 18:1)!

Accept Forgiveness and Give It!

Two evils which the New Testament especially warns disciples about are: (1) the immorality which is so rampant in the heathen world—and which is lightly regarded and (2) the human tendency not to forgive. People find it hard to forgive. They also find it hard to accept forgiveness—to believe that God has forgiven them. And so the New Testament is literally filled with assurances that Christian disciples may claim forgiveness for all their sins and shortcomings through the adequate sacrifice which Jesus made on the cross of Golgotha. He died that we might be forgiven. By our faith in His sacrifice, we are reconciled to the Father. In Him "we have redemption through his blood, the forgiveness of our trespasses, according to the riches of his grace" (Ephesians 1:7). "If we confess our sins, he is faithful and just, and will forgive our sins and cleanse us from all unrighteousness" (1 John 1:9).

There is a price for this forgiveness, however. We must forgive others with the same sort of mercy and compassion which God manifests when He forgives us for Christ's sake. Our Lord gave us a very clear warning on this subject. He told us that if we do not forgive men their trespasses, neither will our Father forgive our trespasses (Matthew 6:14, 15). This is the reason for the tender, earnest exhortation of the Savior: "And whenever you stand praying, forgive, if you have anything against any one; so that your Father also who is in heaven may forgive you your trespasses. But if you do not forgive, neither will your Father who is in heaven forgive your trespasses" (Mark 11:25, 26).

Live as a Forgiven Community

In a profound sense, the church is not so much a community of the best people in the area as it is the community of forgiven and forgiving people. And when sins are forgiven, when they are under the blood of Christ, they should never be mentioned again. Those who committed them will want to, as God does, cast them into the depths of the sea! (Micah 7:19). We who know of their sins will also do as God does. He pardons iniquity and passes by transgression (Micah 7:18). God has promised that as a blessing of the new covenant, He would forgive our iniquity and remember our sin no more (Jeremiah 31:34). The New Testament tells us that we have realized that blessed promise (Hebrews 8:12).

In the Book of Acts, God has given us a good description of the Christian church in its very first decades. We learn there that the disciples cultivated Christian fellowship. They were filled with holy love for God and for one another. They were filled with the joy of forgiven sins, of fellowship with the Father through Jesus Christ, and of fellowship with one another. In their human weakness, they may have tended to live close together instead of going into all the world, as Jesus said, to preach the gospel and make disciples. In the end, a fierce local persecution scattered the early disciples throughout the districts of Judaea and Samaria (Acts 8:1).

Life among the believers before this scattering is a model for the church for all time. With eager joy the early disciples continued steadfastly: (1) in the doctrine of the apostles—that forgiveness and salvation come through faith in the crucified and risen Lord Jesus, (2) in Christian fellowship—celebrating their holy joy and their sense of sharing in the community of faith, (3) in the breaking of bread—frequently celebrating the Lord's Supper as a meal of remembrance, and (4) in the prayers—meeting together to praise God and to bring to Him their supplications and intercessions.

Share Generously

The love and caring among these early disciples was so great that they found it natural to share even possessions. The original Greek in Acts 2:44 reads literally: "And all those believing were together, and they were having all things common, and their properties and possessions they were selling, and they were distributing them to all, according as anyone was having need." Acts 4:32: "Now the multitude of those who believed were of one heart and soul, and not one was saying that anything of the possessions belonging to him [Note that he did own them!] was his own, but all things were common to them." So great was their love that they were most generous in sharing. To them it was not a new legal corporation owning everything, it was a new way to look at the property they owned: Brother A had a need; Brother B had means to help meet that need, so he joyfully gave of his abundance to help his brother. The need of this kind of Christian generosity will always be with us—in all cultures and in all lands.

To own a modest dwelling may be a matter of good stewardship, but to help the needy brother or sister is more important than to accumulate property for "security."

Living as a community of believers is a joyous experience of fellowship in Christ. On the other hand, this community must commission some of the disciples to go into new communities to plant new congregations of believers.

Having one's married brothers and sisters, or married children, living in the immediate geographical area is delightful, but it must not keep us from hearing the call of the Lord to make disciples of all the nations.

Put Your Trust in God

What is the Christian attitude toward the control of crime by the state? The Christian gratefully accepts the "relative security" provided by the police. But the ultimate "security" of the disciple is not in man but in God. Government is, to be sure, one of God's good gifts to mankind, but the Christian does not obey for fear of punishment by the state; he is obedient "for conscience' sake" (Romans 13:5). The Christian disciple puts his real trust not in police protection but in God's providence. Passages such as Psalm 34:6, 7 have always been meaningful and comforting to the people of God:

> This poor man cried, and the Lord heard him,
>   and saved him out of all his troubles.
> The angel of the Lord encamps
>   around those who fear him,
>   and delivers them.

In summary, we have seen that the true Christian disciple patterns his life after Christ. Christ lived love. He lived a holy life. He avoided sin. He lived in trust. He forgave and forgot. He eagerly sought to establish with His disciples a community of forgiven people. He shared generously with those in need and trusted God for His care and protection. These are guidelines for us to follow in the pathway of discipleship.

6

POWER FOR DISCIPLESHIP

CHRISTIAN discipleship doesn't just happen. However, the believer has resources upon which to draw to help him follow Christ each day.

Rest in the Faith

The Christian is a God-centered person. He knows that God loves him with an eternal love. God foreknew him as a believer before the foundation of the world. God chose him in Christ. God predestined him to be conformed to the image of His Son (Ephesians 1).

The Christian knows that God sent His only Son into the world to teach us the truth about the

Father, to show us how to live, love, and trust. He knows that this divine-human being died for our sins on the cross of Golgotha. He knows that His death was an effective sacrifice for our sins, overcoming the devil and all his forces and reconciling us to God.

He knows that the victorious Christ arose from the dead, instructed His apostles for forty additional days, then ascended to the right hand of God where He was enthroned with the Father. This enthroned Christ sent the Holy Spirit upon His waiting disciples on the day called Pentecost, fifty days after Easter (AD 30).

The Christian knows that the Holy Spirit transformed the lives of the early disciples. The Spirit changed them from broken and dispirited men into flaming evangelists and heralds of the good news of the gospel. The believer knows that Christ by His Spirit can deliver anyone from the bondage of sin and bring him into the liberty of the children of God. The Holy Spirit applies the redemption of Jesus to his seeking soul, regenerates him and makes him a partaker of the divine nature. The Holy Spirit makes available to the Christian disciple all the resources of God for deliverance from sin and for victory over the world, the flesh, and the devil. The Spirit transforms him into the spiritual image of his Lord and leads him through life to final victory in the glory world.

Be Filled with the Spirit

The coming of the Holy Spirit to the believer is called the baptism of the Spirit in the New Testament. The baptism of the Spirit is a proof that God has adopted the believer as a son or daughter. The Spirit baptism of the Jewish disciples is recorded in Acts 2. The Samaritans received the Spirit under the ministry of Peter and John, as recorded in Acts 8. And the baptism of believing Gentiles, Cornelius and house, is recorded in Acts 10. Even John the Baptist's disciples had to be baptized with the Spirit when they became Christian disciples (Acts 19). All Christians have the Spirit, for if anyone does not have the Spirit, he is not Christ's disciple (Romans 8:9).

We not only need to repent, believe, and be baptized with the Spirit to become a new creature in Christ and a partaker of the divine nature! We also need to grow, to go on to maturity (called "perfection" in the King James Version), to grow ever more fully into the image of Christ. This growth, this progress in sanctification, cannot be achieved by law. It cannot be achieved by willpower. It cannot be brought about by ceremonies and "sacraments." It cannot be realized by self-denial for the sake of self-denial. Indeed, man cannot achieve "perfection" in his own strength. How then can one become a faithful and effective disciple? The answer of the New Testament is that we need to be *filled* with the Holy Spirit.

Perhaps the greatest statement of the whole New Testament in terms of meeting the conditions for faithful and effective discipleship is Ephesians 5:18. The apostle says we shall not seek temporary stimulation in wine, but "be filled with the Spirit." The English translation cannot give the full meaning of this significant statement.

First of all, there is a "voice" in Greek which is neither active nor passive; it is called the middle voice. It means that one shall take steps to see that something happens. Ananias told Saul, for example, to "be baptized" and "wash away your sins." This is a beautiful illustration of the use of the middle voice. Paul was not to baptize himself, nor was he to just wait for someone to baptize him. He was to see to it that he was baptized, and to make sure that his sins were washed away. In the same way, "be filled" means "see to it that you experience this; meet God's conditions so He can fill you with the Spirit." God's conditions are surrender and faith.

Continue to Be Filled

The other condition for victory is to continue to be filled. And that too is implied in the Greek verb. There is a tense in the imperative which is continuing. So that it means, "Keep on being filled with the Spirit." Today, tomorrow, and every day, "Keep filled!" Keep on yielding to God. Keep your faith fixed on God.

What this really means is that the Christian's blessings are already realized, in one sense, and they are a continuing process on the other hand. Christian experience is both state and process, both already experienced, and yet to be continued. The Christian cannot afford to constantly look back to some outstanding "filling," to some remarkable blessing which the

57

Lord was pleased to bestow in the past. He "forgets" the things of the past in his eagerness to experience greater things. Christian experience is a growing reality. It is always richer on ahead. John Wesley kept urging his believers to seek for what he called "Christian perfection," that is, Christian love in fullness. But he never saw it as an end. "You can," he promised, "grow even more rapidly after you have become perfect in love!"

Rely Upon the Spirit

The Apostle Paul wrote *Ephesians* to Christians at Ephesus and other areas of "Asia" (now Turkey) who needed basic, foundational instruction in Christian living. Paul reminded them that they had already been "sealed" with the Holy Spirit (Ephesians 1:13). The Spirit is God's down payment, marking us as His children, and guaranteeing us the full redemption purchased by Christ when He died for us. (See Ephesians 1:14, 4:30, Romans 8:23.) These disciples at Ephesus had been co-"quickened" [made alive] with Christ, they had co-ascended with Him into the heavenlies, they had even been co-seated with Him! (Ephesians 2:4-6). By this one Spirit, with whom they had been baptized through Christ, they now have access to the Father.

Paul was praying for his readers at Ephesus that they might be strengthened by the Spirit. The Holy Spirit had given them unity. They were in the one body of the church, they were all blessed with the "one Spirit." Paul earnestly urged them not to grieve the Spirit by whom they were sealed (as God's possession) unto the day of redemption—the day when Christ will come in His glory. The Spirit bestows such fruit as goodness, righteousness, and truth. With the Sword of the Spirit, the Word of God, believers can wage a good "war" against sin. The Spirit is the disciple's "Helper." Let's rely upon Him!

Study the Word

Christians receive power through the written Word of God to live the way of discipleship. Jesus said man shall not live by bread alone, but by the Word of God (Matthew 4:4). The Apostle Peter encourages us to desire the sincere milk of the Word that we may grow thereby (1 Peter 2:2). A daily study of God's Word will be a source of daily inspiration and power to the believer. The Holy Spirit also guides and helps the believer to understand the Word.

Pray in Faith

Prayer is perhaps the most unused power in the world. Jesus told His disciples that the prayer of faith could move mountains (Matthew 21:17-22). In the same passage He said whatever believers ask for, *in faith*, they would receive. That's a big promise! Why doubt and live in discouragement when we can pray (1 Timothy 2:8)? Prayer releases the power of God in our lives. Prayer by the believers seems to have had a part in the Apostle Peter's release from prison (Acts 12:1-19). The Apostle James tells us the prayer of faith shall save the one who is sick (5:15). Jesus said men ought always to pray and not to faint

(Luke 18:1). So the true disciple cultivates a life of prayer each day and taps God's unlimited power for daily living.

Bear Fruit

Exercising our muscles makes them stronger. In the same way, bearing the fruit of the Spirit is a source of inspiration and strength to each believer. As each disciple lives love, joy, peace, and the other Spirit fruits (Galatians 5:22), he grows stronger in the faith. Menno Simons said that there is nothing so encouraging as to see the fruit of the Spirit in the lives of Christian disciples. To him, sharing God's good news of the gospel was one of the important fruits of the Spirit. As the disciple lives and shares his faith through the power of the Spirit and the Word, he will grow in Christian discipleship.

7

DISCIPLES SHARE
THE GOOD NEWS

BECAUSE of human nature, believers are tempted to settle back into an easy style of life, satisfied to enjoy eternal life themselves, and hope that their children may also find the way to salvation. Some are tempted to go to church only when convenient, or perhaps only to observe the Lord's Supper. Their names are on the rolls of the church, and what a comfort that is! They give themselves to their secular work to accumulate ever more "security" in preparation for the proverbial "rainy day" (when they cannot work). They give a small amount of their wealth when the church offering is received, and feel that they have done their part. Only rarely is Christ's name heard on their lips, for they feel that anybody can find out about the Christian faith and life if he or she wishes to.

This, however, is not the way of the true disciple of Christ. The genuine disciple wants to exercise his faith very actively and share it with others.

Share Christ Naturally

Sooner or later the Lord will open the way for you to share your faith in a natural way. An opportunity may come your way to talk about your faith to a friend, neighbor, classmate or fellow employee. Or you may want to invite such a person into your home. Christian families may invite a non-Christian family into their home to get better acquainted. Later you may be able to start a Bible study and have prayer together.

Christians are not "pushy" with their faith. Yet, their happiness is so obvious that non-Christians inwardly begin to want what they have. And one day, they too will ask for more formal instruction in the Christian faith, and for water baptism and reception into the church.

Christian Workers Share the Faith

In every community, pastors and other members of the congregation are active in finding new families to have Bible study in their homes. Sometimes women go from house to house to visit and offer practical help. This visitation may be accompanied by a ministry of love, such as supplying medicine for a sick child, or providing milk for a baby. They may offer Christian literature, especially of a practical nature during the visitation. If a neighbor suffers loss through fire or storm, the men help to clean up and rebuild damaged property. Few people are won to Christ unless the Christian worker exercises genuine love. Neither will they become believers if the gospel is not shared with them—in a life of loving service, in printed form, and in glad witness verbally.

Congregations Attract Others

It is most important that every local Christian congregation be a center of happiness and love. If the devil succeeds in making Christians quarrelsome, petty, and jealous, few, if any, non-Christians will be attracted to Christ. But when unselfish love creates a happy Christian fellowship, non-Christians take notice, and if the fellowship reaches out in love and care to others in the community, sooner or later, that church will grow. Individuals and couples will begin to attend the services of the church, and family by family—perhaps several at a time—will begin to confess Christ.

Where this occurs, the church is really being the church. It thus becomes an agency which Christ uses to bring salvation and spiritual life to one person and family after another. The Holy Spirit transforms lives in such a striking manner that the whole community becomes aware of it. It is a blessed experience to be a real disciple, and to be a part of such a happy congregation of Christians.

Evangelists Share Christ

In areas where mass meetings are advisable, an evangelist or experienced minister may conduct a series of evangelistic meetings in a tent, hall, or in the out-of-doors, if the weather permits. This can be an effective way to bring others into Christ's kingdom, especially if Christians bring unsaved to the meetings. It is important that local churches be much involved in such meetings to provide counsel, guidance, and nurture for new believers after the evangelist leaves.

Our Vocation Expresses Christ

The Christian life is not living according to laws, such as in Old Testament times. The Christian is not compelled to behave in a certain way by a set of rules.

Rather, the Holy Spirit makes each new believer a partaker of the divine nature. The New Testament gives the convert practical guidance in becoming a mature Christian and in choosing and carrying out his lifework, so that non-Christians can see Christ in the way he lives. Notice that Christian disciples do not injure their health through drunkenness and wrong use of drugs and other harmful habits. Their friends note their lives of honesty and sobriety—no drunkenness, no immorality, no social dancing, no membership in secret and oathbound societies. And yet Christians—whose lives seem so "tame" to the unconverted—are obviously filled with the joy of the Lord. When such people radiate Christian love and joy in all their contacts, unbelievers come to respect and appreciate them. Many of them are glad to listen to the "secret" of their way of life, and their happiness.

One of the worst mistakes a new Christian can make is to think of Christianity as only a small part of his life. Such a halfhearted Christian lives like a non-Christian much of the time, only he remembers to go to church services occasionally, especially to partake of holy communion. He hopes thereby to maintain salvation and to receive forgiveness for his secular life.

The real Christian disciple, however, sees the new life in Christ as pervading work as well as worship. The factory worker, for example, prays that he may be a clear light for Christ and Christianity in all his new contacts. He does his work so well that everyone can see that he is actually doing his work as unto Christ! The Christian farmer prepares the soil and sows the crop. Then he prays that God may bless the harvest so that his family may have food, with some for the needy. Prayers are made daily for each member of the home so that each may be kept in God's care and be Christlike to others.

Christianity, we repeat, is not a tiny part of an otherwise secular life, rather God through Christ reaches into and makes holy every area of life. None of it is unrelated to God, none of it is actually secular, God is in the whole.

A Holy Life Reveals Christ

The Christian disciple is called with a holy calling—from God through the Spirit. He himself is to be a holy person because he belongs to God, who is holy. He is filled with the Holy

Spirit, who in turn is concerned to make each disciple Christlike. He belongs to a holy body, the body of Christ, the church of the living God. He enters upon full membership in this holy church by holy baptism in which he vows to live a life of holy discipleship. He has a holy Book, sacred Scripture, the Bible. He observes a holy Day, the Lord's Day, in memory of the resurrection of the One who established the church. His very body of flesh and blood is to be kept holy, for it is the Temple of the Holy Spirit. When a couple marries they make holy vows, sacred promises to love one another faithfully until separated by death. They reaffirm these vows daily by living in love and by total self-giving, each to the other.

We need in all our lives an awareness of the holy—not only in times of worship and prayer, but always. When we allow the holy to go out of our life, we become weak and sickly in spirit.

Obstacles to Our Witness

Undoubtedly the greatest dangers to disciples are spiritual coldness and carelessness. The New Testament has much to say about being careful and watchful. The flesh (human nature with its downward pull) tends to neglect prayer, Bible reading, quiet times alone, and fellowship with other Christians. Temptations become very strong for the one who is not careful to keep his Christian experience alive and growing.

The first hazard is therefore lukewarmness. When people become spiritually lukewarm they first lose their spiritual life within, while their external pattern of life may not immediately

66

show it. Then they become an easy prey to spiritual pride. Instead of remaining humble and broken, deeply aware of their constant need of grace, they begin to think of themselves as better than others. After all, they do not carouse, get drunk, and establish immoral relationships. Such spiritual pride is the mark of a cold heart. It was the great sin of the Pharisees, whom the Lord rebuked severely. So let's beware of lukewarmness and spiritual pride.

Victorious Living Expresses the Gospel

These temptations and spiritual hazards can all be avoided by the means of grace God has given. As already noted, these include:

1. "Feeding" (reading and meditating) on the Word of God: "Practice these duties, devote yourself to them, so that all may see your progress" (1 Timothy 4:15)

2. Engaging in earnest prayer, including much thanksgiving, adoration, supplication, and intercession, aware that we need such prayer ourselves. The cause of Christ flourishes to the degree that God's people uphold it in prayer. Further, God is Himself pleased by this "incense" which daily rises to Him (Revelation 5:8).

3. Drawing spiritual courage, strength, and deeper insights from the common life of the saints together: Believers need each other, and they can help one another by mutual affirmation, confession, and forgiveness. The Lord wishes to make each local assembly a discerning body.

4. Being alert to opportunities to share Christ

and His glory with those who do not as yet know Him. Witnessing strengthens the one giving the witness.

5. Practicing sacrificial stewardship—that is, giving generously according to your means. Don't do it with any sense of merit, but as a joyous response to God's goodness and grace.

Disciples Have Concern for the Whole Person

Sometimes well-meaning Christians say that the only reason we need to take food to the starving, build homes for the destitute, provide medical care for the sick, or operate schools for the underprivileged is to lead them to Christ and His salvation. Believers do have the salvation of others as their highest concern. But as stated, it sounds as though Christian disciples take advantage of the weakness of the non-Christians to put pressure on them to become Christians. It sounds as though all that we really care about is that people come into the church.

This is simply not true. Christian disciples have genuine concern for the total well-being of their fellow human beings. It is Christian to provide food and drink for the hungry and thirsty. It is Christian to rebuild dwellings after a tornado, a flood, or a fire. It is Christian to provide medicine and health care for the sick. It is Christian to operate schools to lead persons out of the darkness and fears of ignorance and to bring them into a new world of knowledge and truth.

All of these services could of course be rendered by those who are not themselves Christian disciples. But we are speaking of disciples rendering these services "In the name of Christ." This is the phrase which best expresses the worldwide relief and humanitarian service of the Mennonite Central Committee.

Disciples Are Agents of "Peace"

In their hearts, all genuine Christians long to do what they can to bring spiritual healing and well-being ("Peace" or "Salvation") to those not yet in the kingdom. Providing food, clothing, medicine, and education "In the name of Christ" often gives us an opportunity to share the good news of the gospel.

A government official in a land which did not allow direct evangelism said to a medical doctor, "You are aware, are you not, that you are not allowed to do religious work in this land?"

The doctor replied, "And you are no doubt aware that wherever there are Christians, others are inclined to also become Christians?"

"I am fully aware of it," replied the official!

That is what discipleship is all about—living and sharing Christ in our daily walk of life. It is living under a new authority, the lordship of Christ.

FOR FURTHER STUDY

Harold S. Bender. *The Anabaptist Vision*, Herald Press, Scottdale, Pa., 1966

⸻. "Discipleship," in the *Mennonite Encyclopedia*, Mennonite Publishing House, Scottdale, Pa., Volume IV, 1076, 1077.

⸻. "The Anabaptist Theology of Discipleship," in the *Mennonite Quarterly Review*, XXIV (1950), 25-32.

J. Lawrence Burkholder. "The Anabaptist Vision of Discipleship," in the *Recovery of the Anabaptist Vision*, Herald Press, 1957

Robert Friedman. *Theology of Anabaptism*, Herald Press, 1973

Franklin H. Littell. *Origins of Sectarian Protestantism: The Anabaptist View of the Church*, Macmillan, New York, 1964

Mennonite Confession of Faith, Herald Press, 1963. See Article 16 especially.

John W. Miller. *The Christian Way*, Herald Press, 1969

J. C. Wenger is professor of Historical Theology in Goshen Biblical Seminary, a school of the Associated Mennonite Biblical Seminaries, Elkhart, Indiana. He has made a lifelong study of Anabaptism and has published numerous articles and books in the field.

He studied at Eastern Mennonite and Goshen colleges (BA), at Westminster and Princeton Theological seminaries and at the universities of Basel, Chicago, Michigan (MA in Philosophy), and Zurich (ThD).

He has taught at Eastern Mennonite and at Union Biblical (India) seminaries, and has served on the Committee on Bible Translation which prepared the *New International Bible*.

He is a member of the Evangelical Theological Society. He has served on the editorial boards of the *Mennonite Quarterly Review*, of *Studies in Anabaptist and Mennonite History*, and of the *Mennonite Encyclopedia*, and on the executive council of the Institute of Mennonite Studies.

He has served the Mennonites as a deacon, a minister, and a bishop. He has been a member of their Historical Committee, Publication Board, Board of Education, district and general conference executive committees, and of the Presidium of the Mennonite World Conference.

He married the former Ruth D. Detweiler, RN, in 1937. They are the parents of two sons and two daughters.

A familiar sight in his home city of Goshen is J.C. riding his bicycle on a local errand.